Piranhas

By Sam Dollar

Steadwell
Books

Raintree Steck-Vaughn Publishers

A Harcourt Company

Austin · New York
www.steck-vaughn.com

ANIMALS OF THE RAIN FOREST

Published by Raintree Steck-Vaughn Publishers,
an imprint of Steck-Vaughn Company.

Library of Congress Cataloging-in-Publication Data
Dollar, Sam.
    Piranhas/by Sam Dollar.
        p.cm.--(Animals of the rain forest)
    Includes index.
    ISBN 0-7398-3102-X
    1. Piranhas--Juvenile literature. [1. Piranhas.] I. Title. II. Series.

QL638.C5D66 2000
597.48–dc21

                      00-033814

Printed in the United States of America
10 9 8 7 6 5 4 3 2 1 LB 02 01 00

Produced by Compass Books

Photo Acknowledgments

Tom Brakefield/CORBIS, cover
Ben Klaffke, 4–5, 11, 14, 22, 29
Photophile/Anthony Mercieca, title page
Root Resources/Mary and Lloyd McCarthy, 25, 26
Visuals Unlimited, 8; Rob & Ann Simpson, 12; Kjell B. Sandved, 16

Content Consultant
Bill Lamar
Field Naturalist and Herpetologist

Contents

Caribbean
Sea

VENEZUELA

GUYANA

North
Atlantic
Ocean

SURINAME

FRENCH
GUIANA
(FRANCE)

COLOMBIA

ECUADOR

AMAZON RIVER

PERU

BRAZIL

BOLIVIA

South
Pacific
Ocean

CHILE

PARAGUAY

URUGUAY

South
Atlantic
Ocean

ARGENTINA

Range of the Piranhas

A Quick Look at Piranhas

What do piranhas look like?
Piranhas (puh-RAH-nahs) are meat-eating fish with sharp teeth.

Where do piranhas live?
Piranhas live in South America. They live in the waters of the rain forest.

What do piranhas eat?
Most kinds of piranhas eat meat. Some also eat fruits and nuts.

Do piranhas have any enemies?
Many animals will eat piranhas, especially young piranhas. Birds, caimans, and anacondas hunt piranhas.

Piranhas use their sharp teeth to take bites out of other animals.

Piranhas in the Rain Forest

Piranhas are fish that live in waters of South America. Many piranhas live in the Amazon River. This river flows through Amazonia. Amazonia is the world's largest rain forest. About 1,500 kinds of fish live in rain forest rivers and lakes.

Many people are afraid of piranhas. They have sharp teeth that can bite through skin. Some people believe stories that say piranhas attack and kill people. But most kinds of piranhas do not attack people.

Piranhas are very useful. They are an important food for the people near the Amazon. Piranhas also help clean the waters of the rain forest.

Where Piranhas Live

Like all fish, piranhas are cold-blooded. Cold-blooded animals have blood that is about the same temperature as the air or water around them. Temperature is how hot or cold something is.

Piranhas will die if water becomes too cold. This is why piranhas live in the warmest parts of South America. Piranhas live in warm, low places. Water in the mountains is too cold for piranhas to live.

What Piranhas Look Like

Scientists have found at least 30 kinds of piranhas. Each kind of piranha is a different color. Piranhas can be silver, black, or blue. Some kinds of piranhas have colored spots or red stomachs.

All piranhas have some things in common. They have sharp, triangle-shaped teeth and strong jaws. The lower jaws of many piranhas stick out more than the upper jaws. When piranhas' jaws close, their upper and lower teeth fit together closely. They slide against each other like scissors.

▲ The colorful, hard scales of this red-bellied piranha protect its body like armor.

Most piranhas are oval-shaped and flat. This shape helps them swim fast through water. Piranhas have five kinds of fins. Fins are body parts that help fish swim. The fins work together to help piranhas move and change direction in the water.

A piraya is one kind of large piranha.

Three Kinds of Piranhas

Some larger kinds of piranhas are a danger to people. Black piranhas, red-bellied piranhas, and pirayas are all large piranhas. A group of them could hurt or kill a large animal or person.

Black piranhas are a common kind of piranha. They live mostly in the Amazon River and the Orinoco River. They are black with red eyes. Their powerful jaws are strong enough to bite off a person's finger.

Red-bellied piranhas are one of the most colorful kinds of piranha. They have red throats and stomachs when they are young. The colors become lighter as the fish grow older. They live mostly in lakes.

Pirayas are the largest of all piranhas. Many live in the Sao Francisco River in Brazil. They grow at least 20 inches (51 cm) long or more.

Piranhas bite small chunks of meat out of their prey.

Hunting and Eating

What a piranha eats depends on what kind of piranha it is. Most kinds of piranhas eat meat. They are predators. A predator is an animal that hunts and eats other animals. Prey are animals that are hunted and eaten by predators.

Some kinds of piranhas do not eat much meat. Instead, they eat fruits, nuts, and seeds that fall in the water.

Young piranhas will sometimes eat insects. Adult meat-eating piranhas eat fish. They also eat birds, reptiles, freshwater crabs, and frogs. Some piranhas eat pieces of the fins and tails of other fish. They sometimes bite the toes and tails of swimming animals.

Piranha schools may have from several fish to 100 or more fish.

How Piranhas Hunt

Piranhas have special senses to help them hunt prey. A piranha has four nostrils. Piranhas are drawn to the smell of blood. They use their sense of smell to find bleeding prey. They then attack and eat the bloody prey. Piranhas kill by biting small pieces out of their prey's bodies. Piranhas do not chew their food. They swallow food whole.

Piranhas also have special hairs on their bodies. These hairs sense movement in water. Piranhas can use their hairs to find moving prey.

Piranhas have many different ways of hunting. Piranhas will sometimes hide among plants and rocks until prey comes near. When prey swims close, piranhas will use their strong fins to zoom forward and attack.

Some piranhas live and hunt in groups called schools. One scientist saw a school of piranhas hunting a group of fish. One of the piranhas swam in and scattered the group of fish. Then each piranha attacked a prey fish.

Piranhas sometimes act as scavengers. A scavenger is an animal that eats dead animals that it did not kill itself. Piranhas will eat both dead people and animals. Piranhas help keep rivers clean by eating the dead animals and fish.

You can see the eye-like marking on this colorful peacock cichlid.

Escaping the Predator

Sometimes what a fish looks like helps protect it from piranhas. Peacock cichlids and oscars are kinds of fish that often escape piranhas. These fish have a mark near the tail that looks like an eye. Scientists believe the "eye" fools piranhas. They often do not attack peacock cichlids and oscars.

Fish that have red coloring on their bodies sometimes escape piranha attacks, too. Many piranhas also have some red coloring on their bodies. The piranhas might be tricked into thinking the prey is another piranha. For example, the red-bellied pacu looks like the red-bellied piranha. This helps protect the pacu from piranha attacks.

Sometimes fish fight back against piranhas. A group of fish may swim toward a piranha and chase it away. Cichlid fish may form a circle. They keep their tail fins pointing toward the center of the circle. This stops piranhas from biting off pieces of the cichlids' tail fins.

Anacondas often swim through the water to hunt for piranhas and other prey.

A Piranha's Life Cycle

Scientists have a difficult time studying piranhas in the wild because the fish live underwater. The waters of the rain forest are filled with many predators, such as crocodile-like caimans and giant snakes called anacondas. This makes it unsafe to study piranhas.

Scientists are not sure how piranhas mate and reproduce. Most scientists believe piranhas mate during the rainy season. It rains almost every day during this time. Water in rivers and lakes rises and floods the forest floor.

The flooded forest is an important food for young piranhas. The young swim into the flooded forest and eat fruits and nuts.

Spawning

Female piranhas spawn. Spawning means laying large amounts of eggs. No one knows where wild piranhas spawn. Some scientists think piranhas make nests on muddy river bottoms. Other scientists think females lay eggs on plants.

Scientists study how piranhas in aquariums spawn. In aquariums, some female piranhas lay their eggs on the bottom of the tank. Other aquarium piranhas make a nest of water plants. They clean a special spot with their fins. Then they lay their eggs on the plants. The eggs stick to the plants.

Eggs hatch about four days after females lay them. Young piranhas break out of the eggs. These piranhas are called fry.

◄ **These young fry are about three weeks old. They are a few inches long.**

Growing Piranhas

Young fry are weak and small. They are less than 1 inch (about 2 cm) long when they hatch. Birds, turtles, snakes, caimans, or other fish eat many young piranhas. Few live to become adults.

Sometimes adult piranhas help keep fry safe from predators. But many fry are left to take care of themselves. They spend most of their time among the stems and roots of plants. Piranhas hide in the plants so predators cannot see them. The fry also swim through the plants looking for food.

When fry grow larger, they leave the plants and hunt small fish. Then they return to hide in the plants at night.

Piranhas grow during their entire lives if they have enough food. As they grow older, they do not grow as quickly. But they still grow. Most piranhas grow to be 10 to 12 inches (25 to 30 cm) long. They live for 5 to 10 years.

This caiman is eating a red-bellied piranha.

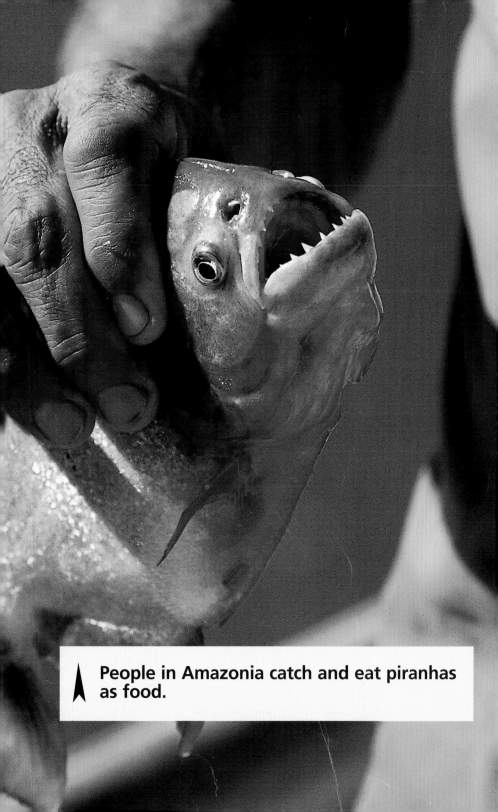

People in Amazonia catch and eat piranhas as food.

Living with Piranhas

Scientists disagree about how much of a danger piranhas are to people. There is no proof that piranhas have ever killed people. In fact, many people in Amazonia safely swim in rivers and lakes that are full of piranhas.

Most piranha bites on people happen by accident. Piranhas bite people who are fishing. Piranhas may bite when they are pulled out of the water. People fishing have lost toes and fingers this way.

Piranhas are most unsafe during the dry season when little rain falls. The rivers and lakes that piranhas live in sometimes become dry. Piranhas might run out of food. Then piranhas will eat anything that comes into the water. They will even eat other piranhas.

Useful Piranhas

People of South America have been living near piranhas for a long time. They eat piranhas as food. People in these places have used piranha jaws as cutting tools.

Piranhas are an important part of the rain forest. They help keep the rivers free of dead fish. Dead fish can poison the water. Piranhas sometimes spread the seeds that they eat. The seeds can grow new rain forest plants.

Some people do not understand how useful piranhas are. They kill large numbers of piranhas by poisoning them. These people kill piranhas because the piranhas make fishing difficult. Piranhas' strong teeth can bite through fishing nets or fishhooks.

Scientists do not know what will happen if people keep poisoning piranhas. Piranhas and all living things work together to keep the rain forest healthy. Loss of piranhas could hurt the rain forest.

Young piranhas are food for many predators in the rain forest.

Glossary

cold-blooded (kohld-BLUHD-id)—having blood that is about the same temperature as the air or water

fin (FIN)—a special body part that helps fish change direction and swim

predator (PRED-uh-ter)—an animal that hunts and eats other animals

prey (PRAY)—animals that are hunted by other animals for food

scales (SKALES)—the small, protective plates covering a fish's body

scavenger (SCAV-un-jer)—an animal that eats dead animals that it did not kill

school (SKOOL)—a group of fish

spawn (SPAWN)—to lay a large number of eggs

Internet Sites and Addresses

The Discovery Channel
http://www.discovery.com

Piranha.Org
http://www.piranha.org

Rain Forest Alliance
http://www.rainforest-alliance.org

Defenders of Wildlife
1101 Fourteenth Street, NW #1400
Washington, DC 20005

Fish Unlimited
P.O. Box 1073
Shelter Island Heights, NY 11965

Index